Maz

J D Swan-De La Mazière

Contents

Foreword.

It's time to hear it like it is, the truth in all its glory. It's time we stopped pretending that everything is ok now we have anti-discrimination laws, and that the bad times have passed.

It's time that a working-class voice gave a different slant on this situation.

This is not for self-pity, this is for everyone who can't get over what happened, to have their voices heard. It is just my story, amongst thousands of others. I don't claim to speak for all the other veterans who went through this, but I will tell it like it is.

J D Swan-De La Mazière

Able Rating

W139913R

Acknowledgements.

To all my partners and employers of the past, to those who have sat and listened, to Andie my wife, and to my Mum on the other side: thank you for being there, thank you for helping me make sense of the journey, however long it has taken, and for putting up with it all.

To all those who know nothing of this dirty little secret of British Military History, I hope you find this an eye-opener.

To all my oppos and shipmates, thanks for not putting the boot in. Bravo Zulu.

Thanks to Dr Jo Stanley for being the first person to include me in something seafaring since my dismissal – the Sailing Proud Archive at Merseyside Maritime Museum, and for helping to share this book around.

Cheers to Helen, Annie, Adam, Gillian, Niall, and Von, for giving us the lowdown on book publishing, ideas, or helping with editing. I owe you a bevy.

Thankyou to the Kop Outs and United with Pride, for welcoming me into a different uniformed family; that of the football community.

'A job in the Naval service means adventure, camaraderie, and lifelong prospects. Every day you make a difference. And no two days are the same....are you ready to go places?'

www.royalnavy.mod.uk

Razor Blades.

Razor Blades – The end of a ship's life, and the recycling of its parts into usable artefacts.

..-. ..- -.-. -- - .... —

"Fuck this shit" I spelled out in Morse code, over and over as I sat in the December air of Dunfermline, HM Forces rail warrant in hand, black canvas kit bag holding a few precious reminders of what might have been; my cap tallies, my beret badge, and a few uniform badges; at least mine weren't ripped from my uniform, unlike those of others.

At 21, I learned that the country I had stepped forward to serve, didn't want me.

This is my true dit…

Launch.

Launch – a ceremony when a new ship is first introduced to the water.

I was born into poverty and I'm still in it. My Mum never went to school, forced through circumstance to sleep in potato sacks, look after her two disabled Brothers and watch her Dad bring women home from around the streets of Liverpool, whilst her Mum worked in manual jobs.

Mum was eighteen when she'd had me, my Dad was seventeen. This was the early seventies. Liverpool was riding the boom of the swinging sixties, the Merseybeat and musical revival. They'd met in the furniture department of Owen Owen's department store. Then came me, conceived in the sand-dunes of the Sefton coast during 1970, born in 1971. Links to the sea started early!

After that followed my brother, and soon after, Thatcher, who brought the managed decline we both felt. We shared books in freezing, temporary classrooms, our NHS glasses held together with Sellotape, our holey shoe soles supplemented by cardboard, enduring the indignity of free school meals.

I was keen and bright, and in every after-school club there was, but often bullied for being a swot. Unknown to me then, university was never going to be on the cards, not for someone from the poverty of income, aspiration, and culture that I came from.

Then there was the Sea Cadets: sunset nights of this younger teenager rowing on the Manchester Ship Canal, learning radio communications and chatting to the passing tugs, and playing snare drum up and down the road in practice parades. It provided an escape from the poverty fuelled rages at home, the surviving on stolen vegetables that my Mum, Nin and Granddad Paddy had nicked from farmers' fields, and the lack of family holidays. Sea Cadets gave me something else too – a love of the sea, a knowledge of how to polish boots, and an introduction to Naval traditions.

At fifteen, the desperation of long-term unemployment drove my Dad to take a job in a butcher's shop that came with a house – in rural Oxfordshire. Right in the middle of fucking nowhere.

The daily minibus pickups were full of privileged twats who gleefully tormented us for our accents, and burst into Beatles songs as we boarded. I'd lost my chances of good exam grades, as there was no national curriculum then, despite my hard work. I'd also lost my friends and hobbies. This was just the start of a repeating life pattern of familiarity and of prospects being taken from me.

Forced to re-sit some of my 'O' levels, I went to a college in Stratford-Upon-Avon. I was a bit of an oddity, being a working-class Northerner, amongst fresh faced teenagers whose parents bought them cars or horses for passing their exams. It was like something of a social experiment. Luckily, the dropout rockers, goths, scooter gangs and teenage pissheads I seemed to bond with, saved me from isolation. We had lunchtime riverside ciders, music, and volunteer drumming lessons for the local disabled kids that were shipped to the college once a week.

I studied sociology at the college, never considering that one day, I might well be part of the syllabus. I wanted to pursue sociology at 'A' Level, but we were moved again. My Dad took another job in another county, due to bullying at work. But at least I was bought a drum kit on credit with the surplus he brought in.

After a dripping summer working in a bakery wearing a plastic apron, watching maggots falling from the factory mop (something I later reported as a health and safety concern), it was clear to me that I was going nowhere in life, I headed into my nearest big city - Coventry - and joined the Royal Navy.

Bizarrely, I'd already made two friends in Coventry. I later found out that both of them were gay, but I was too naïve to know that back then.

"At least I know the ranks and badges from the Sea Cadets," I told myself as I heaved open the careers office door bedecked with posters of vessels and uniforms.

"Are you a communist?" barked the recruiting officer.

"No."

In truth, I didn't even know what one was. Weren't they supposed to be Russian?

"Are you a homosexual?"

"No."

My only understanding of what a homosexual was, had been gleaned from my Dad, telling me that all shirt-lifters ponce around in shorts; they hang round in public toilets, carrying AIDS. His 1989 version was no doubt fuelled by the foreboding adverts on TV about the virus. The only other homosexual I knew about was John Inman in "Are you being served?"

A fitness test followed, then a few weeks later an oath to the Queen with my innocent hand on the bible, at Birmingham New Street careers office. And there I was, ship-shape and Bristol fashion: A member of the Women's Royal Naval Service. A wren.

I wanted to go in as a weapons analyst. But they said there shortages, so I had opted to be a radio operator instead. That put my existing knowledge from the cadets, to good use. In all honesty, I just wanted to play on boats and play drums. I was pretty pissed off when I later found out that only rare Wrens ever managed to get afloat and that it was the Royal Marines (then males-only) who got to play the drums.

"What yer doin in six weeks Mum?"

I asked as she stood over the frying pan, egg and chips on the go.

"Dunno. Why?"

"Well, it'll be my passing out parade"

"Wha?"

"I've joined the Navy Mum"

"Yer aven't!"

"I have!"

Who knows what ran through her mind. She was worried sick, no doubt, about finding the money to get to Devon. What was running through my mind of course, were the chances I'd never get at home – study, travel, three meals a day, a career, and a roof over my head.

Over the years, many gay women I've met have assumed that all women join the forces because we're fascist, egoistical and/or thick. I was none of those things, I was poor. If the lottery of birth had given me parents with fatter wallets and outlooks, things may have been different.

"Wait til yer Dad finds out" she said.

He on the other hand, seemed delighted. One of us was off his hands and therefore there was one less to worry about.

So, 4th December 1989, I travelled from Rugby to Plymouth, clutching my Mum's 'docker' sandwiches in tightly packed foil, not even the re-used stuff she normally used. She stood with tears in her eyes, my brother watching wide-eyed and my Dad gleefully and mockingly saying "bye bye".

I was half shitting myself, half excited.

Six weeks later, my brother joined up too, possibly as a blow to my Dad who had been a soldier in the King's Regiment of the Territorial Army. He now had two kids in the Royal Navy and his Dad, with whom he'd never bonded, was ex-Merchant Navy. I never knew how my Dad actually felt about this, but I did wonder if it is why he would put my brother down at every opportunity.

As we got closer to Dawlish Warren, the scenery, and my mind, opened up. Crashing waves and steep cliffs. A foreboding. The few remaining female passengers, started chatting, as we realised we were all heading the same way. We must be fledgling Wrens!

That was the start of it – Hermes 49 Division at HMS Raleigh. The initial boot camp for all naval ratings. What a motley crew. We came from all corners of the UK, from military or broken families, or both. There were a couple of officer types usually from somewhere ending 'shire,' there to do their basic training before heading off to Britannia Royal Naval College in Dartmouth.

What laughs we had too: mud, sweat, cold, heat, tiredness. They all became a second skin that we wore. I had trained and trained to get fit, but nothing could've prepared me for the next level that basic training pushed me to.

There was Natalie from Hartlepool, (not her real name), who had joined the Royal Navy – but couldn't swim. How the hell she did extra swimming lessons on top of basic training, I will never know, but she did it, with the encouragement of the band of sisters we'd become. The first Sister's I'd ever had in my life. Chalkie, a fellow Scouser who shared the same quarters as me, was repeatedly insubordinate and disorganised, to the point of being akin to Private Benjamin. Eventually she got herself discharged for sticking two fingers at a Chief Wren during rounds, having been witnessed by the accompanying inspecting officer.

Christmas leave in 1989 was a blessing for me - I was able to stuff my face back home enough to rebuild some of my lost strength - the demands of training had weakened me, and I had a sore throat coming on. My Mum had got us a large turkey, thankfully.

I went back to base in January 1990, and we were out on a gruelling expedition with the Royal Marines on Dartmoor, in freezing fog and ice.

"Are you taking the fucking piss?" crackled the hand-held radio, the marine clearly furious…

We were nestled in the unforgiving openness, devoid of landmarks for us to anchor ourselves to on the creased, now sodden, maps we were holding. A marine had just asked my unwitting oppo what our next plans were.

"We're spreading out in a bunch, sir"

"You're fucking what?" he demanded

That ended our bottle-green backup. The only time we saw them again was when the marines Land Rover scooped up the blistered and battered amongst us, hauling them off to sick bay.

I'd been appointed as a lead to get us through this demanding exercise. It was tough. People were tired, blistered, some without sleep. Some were struggling with the weight of their bergens. We rotated tasks, helped carry the bergens, and I encouraged us to sing. Singing seemed to stick with us as a way through it all – we'd begged staff at HMS Raleigh to let us play football at times, during which we'd sing "You'll Never Walk Alone" like swaggering terrace ultras, thrashing our opponents. Another time we'd got a serious bollocking for taking the piss at the enforced Christmas church service we were obliged to attend in uniform, during which we entertained ourselves, and the public, with deliberately raucous, footy-esque versions of what should have been a soothing *Away in a Manger*.

We did it across Dartmoor, gleefully bouncing out 'The Gypsy Rover' as we suddenly found the energy to make the last strides up the hill to the local pub.

The bonds formed in training last a lifetime. Any service man or woman will tell you that. I still feel proud of how we encouraged, hugged, praised, bollocked and hauled each other as a group, through this. But prejudice was never far away…

"She's a fucking lesbo that Woody, I'm tellin yer" said Mandy, as she spat on her shoe and rubbed black Kiwi shoe polish into it.

Woody was officer material, older, better educated and far more articulate than us. She was kind too, I recall her talking me through ironing the yolk of a shirt first, in her Queen's English, acquired somewhere not from my background. I didn't know what a yolk was. Something only an egg has, I thought.

I didn't have a fucking clue what a lesbian was either.

"Oh right," I replied.

Mandy clearly knew more of the world than I, and a lesbian was obviously something predatory, to be fearful of, and to look under the bed for before shutting lights out for the night.

I never knew how Woody got on, whether she was indeed a 'lesbo,' but she was certainly ostracised by a few of the division.

Passing Out.

Passing out – a special occasion or parade for newly qualified service men and women.

Nothing short of an understatement, that. Many of us did pass out, after hours on parade, managing to shovel only the first half of our scran down our necks first thing in the Morning, to keep our energy up.

Every single one of us had been put through something that pushed our buttons in those six weeks – heights, water, tunnels, or studying, seemed to be the biggest blockers. Yet we were reconstructed into service women. And then there we were - proud, shining, and knackered.

My Mum, Dad, Brother, and Granddad drove down in my Dad's knackered bronze Ford Cortina, with a loan from the Provy to cover the petrol costs. I will never know where, or if, they slept. Perhaps it was in the car, because they'd have been too skint for a hotel. They looked shattered and could barely afford the glossy official photos of me, or any mementoes from the ship's shop.

I was proud – of myself – something I forget to be nowadays. I was called to receive a prize for endeavour during training – a hardback atlas, and with hundreds of other sailors and Wrens, we marched behind the Royal Marines band for our final passing out parade at HMS Raleigh. But as we turned the final corner as to march past the dais for the final salute – it pissed down.

We couldn't fucking believe it. We'd been stood there for hours, fainting or tired, and here we were, the raindrops bouncing off our white caps.

I do often wonder if the universe rained on my parade as a signal.

And signals it was, for the next stage of training was at the Royal Naval Communications School – HMS Mercury in Petersfield, Hampshire.

Bidding farewell to the steel bunk beds and 1970s striped blankets of HMS Raleigh, we said our goodbyes to those heading to different branches of the Royal Navy, and all headed out of Devon. Trade training was less demanding, accommodation rooms were smaller, we were allowed our own duvets even, and we had time for a drink.

I immersed myself in the machines and art, of morse code, touch typing, signal classifications and structures. HMS Mercury was also, the first, and last, time I had a boyfriend. I never knew why I lacked my Shipmates' enthusiasm for men. We all had a boyfriend at HMS Mercury, and mine was Ste, (not his real name), from the North East. We'd all head off to the seaside on the Isle of Wight at weekends off. Thankfully we drank so much that nothing got further than some desperate fumbling – by him.

HMS Mercury had its own laughs too. I was often partnered with a Northern Irish Wren Lisa, not her real name. As a couple, the 'Paddy and the Scouser,' we'd often be summoned to the regulators – the Naval Police - usually over some witnessing of a late-night incident at the oggy van. There were Friday night runs on the battered Royal Navy bus, into Petersfield, a small town square where a segregation of civvy versus Navy pubs became a central, late-night battlefield. Segregation! Regulators would often be baton-handed as they separated the guilty parties and their inebriated shipmates. Back they sent us, onto the bus, for the inevitable captain's table and ensuing punishment, the following day.

Daytimes, back at Mercury, parades and inspections were an outlet for fun and misdemeanour. Many of us stifled giggles as the weeks, and passing officers, went by.

At one point we had an inspection by a member of the Royal family, during which my oppo 'Choppy,' a balding male sailor festooned with customary tattoos, had asked her for a cigarette and informed her that on cold days such as this, he wished Nelson would've lost at the battle of Trafalgar. He was later seen in only his underpants, running round the parade ground with a toilet seat round his neck, telling passers-by that he was "shithouse of the week."

I also recall a botched attempt to replace the taped, default parade practice music - 'Hearts of Oak,' with the theme tune from the TV comedy show Monty Python's Flying Circus. Had it been achieved; I am not sure how many of us would have managed to successfully stifle the smirks as the guard marched past.

I passed out of HMS Mercury in May 1990, My Mum and Dad in attendance. Many went for drinks and dinners with families afterwards, my family walked to the local village pub, the Rising Sun in East Neon, for half a lager, it was all that they could afford.

Underway.

Underway – the movement of a boat through water.

"Just fuckin chuck it Maz" yelled Sharky at me as we stood at the top of the stairs In Baker Street tube station, unable to haul all our uniform and cases in one go.

Maz was my Navy nickname. Anyone in the forces has a nickname, usually based around your surname or some other characteristic. We had 'Tiny' – a 6'7" physical training instructor, black people were often called 'Snowy', those with the surname Adams were called 'Fanny', Coopers were called 'Mini', Webbs 'Spider', Bells 'Dinger' and Whites 'Chalkie'…you get the idea. I often felt for the Northern Irish amongst us, who were repeatedly nicknamed 'Semtex', in a nod to the explosive used by the Irish Republican Army against British occupying troops.

Chuck it I did, my standard issue Royal Navy suitcase hurtling down the stairs with a pile of others, and dragged onto the tube to Northwood in Middlesex – our first real posting – HMS Warrior. This was a NATO base staffed with international forces, Royal Navy, and RAF personnel together were all doing their bit for the Gulf War effort, August 1990 – February 1991.

It was exciting; doing the job you had been trained to do, handling classified material and in a real-life scenario. It was exciting for another reason too. This was where I realised I was gay.

I was placed in a block with mixed WRAF and WRNS. It was a dimly lit but warm place, with huge washing machines you had to queue for, a TV room and dark corridors. I shared a room with three other Wrens, all on the same shift '- 'D' Watch. Jane – not her real name, was someone I would see around a lot, at work, in the galley and in the block. She had dark, curly hair, glinting brown eyes and a naughty smile. She was definitely, one of the naughty crew, hosting late night beer drinking sessions, and reflective, spiritual, alcohol-fuelled chats. My crush on her strengthened as I go to know her. She knew it, often sitting late at night, eyeing me, and awaiting me to get the bottle up to say something.

"I, I fancy you love" I blurted one night.

"Maz, I know. Problem is, I have a girlfriend."

The sinking feeling was like someone had pressed the down button in the lift. I was stunned and pissed off, but I accepted, and listened.

Her girlfriend it turned out, was Katy, another Wren, also from my neck of the woods in the North West. Katy was as butch as fuck.

When I first saw her, she looked like a bag of burglar's tools. My 19-year-old lustful self, couldn't understand why she was a higher rank in the looks stakes than I. I had confidence back then; the Navy instil it into you.

Katy eventually got wind of my little crush, and warned me off, but equally assured me that all was fine. My friendship with the two of them shaped into weekend nights at The Bell, a key lesbian and gay pub in Kings Cross.

The ensuing months cemented my acknowledging to myself that I was gay. The women I saw at The Bell looked like me, dressed like me on my days off, and so a whole new world revealed itself.

I desperately wanted to tell someone, anyone. I wanted to talk through the passing, unregistered hurt of Jane. But in all honesty, I still wasn't fully sure of myself. What was I supposed to do in bed? At what point did a crush become my identity, a label? Was I even gay?

I couldn't tell my colleagues. No chance. I couldn't even go sick and have the stigma of a mental or personality disorder attached to me, and I certainly couldn't tell the chaplain; he would be duty-bound to grass me up.

Unbeknown to me, during that time, Jane and Katy were put under surveillance by the SIB – the Special Investigation Branch, the detective arm of the Military Police. This was part of a witch-hunt of thousands of service men and women that lasted between the 1940s and 2000, especially as part of the Cold War.

HMS Warrior inadvertently ensured that off-duty, I enjoyed months of highs and lows, laughs and alcohol, as I bounced round my new identity. 'D' watch were a top crew of Royal Navy and RAF, all proud, hardworking, and professional. Credit to them for the nights in the Commcen – the Communications Centre - we spent during Operation Desert Shield.

We would go on all night drinking sessions, doing the entire Circle line of the London tube, singing in pubs in dodgy areas, even ending up one night in an Irish pub in Kilburn when the curtains were shut, and the bucket sent round for 'the cause.' We duly chipped in.

I loved being on guard duty on the main gate too. Now it would be totally inappropriate, but then my Royal Marines mates were a laugh; they'd take the piss out of anyone and everyone. Often, we'd play snooker together – that was the act of searching different coloured cars matching the colour and order of a game of snooker, arriving at the main gate, for bombs. Often we would deliberately target officer ranks, just for the fun of frustrating them as they arrived late for a meeting. The marines would also chop up a smoked sausage, and chuck pieces of it at some of the quieter Wrens on their way in or out of the main gate. They'd then set an Alsatian on the Wrens, just to see the women's reaction.

Some nights in the Commcen were eerie. Signal traffic was low, and we were there to support the fleet, but we didn't know what was happening to them, so far away in the Gulf. One minute we would be talking to them, the next minute, silence.

We felt helpless, back on a base, not knowing if they'd been hit. We just had to wait, and so we'd spend time reading, studying, or playing with the Fuzzy-Felt we'd bought in bulk from Hamley's toy store. It was during one similar night that I decided to nip off to the vending machine to get a coffee. That's how I met Maureen – not her real name, my second crush.

Maureen was a radar operator, the same branch as me – operations. Believe me, I would have loved to have been on operations with her! Sadly, it was never meant to be. This was despite my best attempts to visit her with flowers when she was bedridden in sick bay, to 'happen' to be in the TV room at the same time she was, and to pretend to tie my shoe laces when she passed by me – only to realise I was wearing slip-ons.

I did almost get there mind. One day she opened her door and thanked me for the flowers. She turned round to look amongst the old wooden wardrobes, and was about to kiss me, when a door in the corridor clicked further down. Instead she got cold feet, and I got wet knickers.

It transpired that Maureen lived with another Wren, an officer, and was estranged from her parents. They had to be secretive or else they would both lose their careers. So, by now, I'd had two crushes on women. It was clear to me that I was "one of them" – a shirt lifter, lesbo, dirty lezzer, rug muncher, pussy licker, poof, queer, shit-stabber, faggot.

I had to tell someone. Sharky and I had headed into London many a time, once to get tattoos done, proper Navy-style. This time we were sat on the pavement with a jacket potato in Covent Garden, looking forward to listening to the dodgy recordings of gigs we'd got from the nearby record shop. I told her I was gay.

"Yer know what Maz? I don't give a fucking fuck! You're my mate and oppo, and that's it" she said in her broad Wigan accent.

So, there it was, my coming out, my big moment reduced to a few seconds of hot polystyrene and melted cheese.

Inspired by this acceptance, I decided to tell my closest shipmates, who had organised a jolly down to Southend beach. As we sat in the sand, I unfurled my story, and the chatter and sunshine, slowed. None of them had an issue with it. But I felt it necessary to explain my journey, and the fact I didn't fancy any of them, which was the truth. They were visibly relieved when I mentioned it. In an incredible act of warmth and compassion, they gathered round me, and hugged and assured me that it would all be OK. I will never forget that roller coaster of a day. It was clear that they would have my back, as much as I would have theirs.

As the years have gone by, it has always amazed me how the stereotyped, prejudiced policies at the time, bore no resemblance to the actual lived experience or views, of many of those in boots on the ground. Their attitude was "well you're one of ours, so what? We're still a division, still there for each other, no matter what."

My time at HMS Warrior also exposed to me the double standards that were applied to homosexual versus heterosexual, personnel. The bottom line is, rules were rules. Yet I saw groups of Royal Marines turn up at the bar in drag, pretending to give each other a blow job and masturbating onto a digestive biscuit; this was a regular competition apparently: the last one to come had to eat the biscuit. One of the women in my room often had her boyfriend stay the night, against regulation. These offences went unsupervised or ignored, whilst the sexual equivalent of having the wrong eye or hair colour, was zealously punished by those in charge.

The Trots.

Trots – a loose bowel movement or diarrhoea.

It was a quiet night and so I had a stand-off. This is where lower ranks like me would be allowed to finish their shift early but had to stay dressed in 8's – fire party uniform, in case of an emergency, for the rest of their shift. It meant you could get some kip. Tonight, was my turn, around March 1990, I can never recall the exact date, and the Ministry of Defence and Royal Navy, both had conveniently 'lost' records of what happened, when I requested them years later.

I was alone and asleep in my room, when something disturbed me. Something heavy on top of me. I awoke to find an Alsatian on top of my bed. Next to it, a male warrant officer and two women I did not recognise from the base, one in WRAF and one in WRNS uniform.

"Get up Wren Maz. Stand by your bed" one of them ordered. I did.

What happened over the next few hours, changed my life, my self-esteem, and my mental health, forever.

With my back stood to my pit, the two unknown women proceeded to search my belongings. Everything got turned over or out, pockets in my uniform, behind my posters, inside my union-jack duvet cover, books, laundry. Nothing got spared.

"What's this?" one glared at me as she quizzically held up the tarot cards I had bought myself.

"Tarot cards" I replied, thinking "What a thick cow you are. It's fucking obvious what it is."

"Are you a witch?" she followed. "I wish" I thought to myself. She followed by holding up some incense sticks I'd stuck in my musky wardrobe to brighten the smell. Did this lot not have anything better to do, I wondered, like defending our country for example?

Before I could answer she stated, "Do you know that incense is used to disguise the smell of drugs?"

"No" I answered. That's the truth. I didn't. Nor have I ever taken drugs in my entire life, bar the drug of choice in HM Forces – booze – everyone's bezzy and confidante. It did cross my mind to wonder why the SIB would concentrate on some drugs, but not the biggest drug used daily by pretty much most people in the services.

So, there I was, within 20 minutes, I'd gone from being an able rating to a drug-taking, Scouse witch.

She then spied the tattoo…

"Why have you got a tattoo on your left shoulder?" she barked

"Cos that's where I felt it looked best" I retorted.

Unbeknown to me, having a tattoo on your left shoulder was apparently, the lesbian equivalent of Polari or the gay men's handkerchief code – a true sign you were a lesbian. She proceeded by asking me what rings I had, or was wearing. Did I have a black onyx ring? I didn't but I learned years later that that too, worn on your pinkie finger, was a code used by gay women in the forces. I wish I'd known; I would have gone and got myself one so I could pull!

I was then handcuffed, and marched in shame down the long, dark corridor of my block, past shipmates coming in from the night shift. This must have been around 0730 hours. At 51 years old now, the memories of what happened to the 19-year-old me are still a blur.

I was taken somewhere underground – the Commcens were all underground. I was put in a plain office with just one desk and three chairs. There were no items on the cork noticeboard I could see, and no clock. My chair was pulled back deliberately from the table, so I couldn't reach it for comfort. Then it started, eighteen hours of interrogation. No food, no water, nobody there with me, no legal representation, no phone call home allowed. Nothing.

They played good cop, bad cop, with one staring right in front of me, while the other paced behind me, screaming in my ear. The constant roar of "I don't fucking believe you" I can still hear today.

"How do you have sex?"

"Do you use sex toys?"

"Do you fancy your Mum?"

"Do you look at your mates in the showers?"

"How many fingers do you put inside a woman?"

"Have you ever kissed Jane?"

"When you sit on the bed with an oppo, do you have at least one of your feet on the floor?"

"Are you or aren't you?"

This went on and on, and frankly, was terrifying. I had no idea how lesbians have sex. It was frightening and overwhelming, and looking back, based on shocking stereotypes or perceptions, of what women do or don't do, in bed. I know of gay men who do not have anal sex, but plenty of straight couples that do, yet the stereotyping persists to this day does it not? Imagine if this was your daughter, sister, Mum or friend, being asked this by strangers.

Then my address book was presented like a prize, and I was forced to turn each page, describing who my friends and family were, and whether they were gay. I was spat at, I had board rubbers thrown at me and was humiliated as a human being. I was made to feel inadequate, less than worthy of being in the WRNS, dirty, ashamed. All this was at a critical time of development in anyone's life, their teens, and early twenties, and all at a time when I hadn't even kissed a woman.

I was in tears and emotionally and physically drained. The warrant office re-appeared, and that is when I remembered something. His son Nick was on the same base as me at the time, and I had been at a party with him in a marines block a few weeks earlier.

"I'm not gay" I declared, "Ask him – I was at a party with his son." It's true that the buzz was that I was a bit of a slapper, being seen at various parties.

I will never know if that's what got me off the hook or not, I can only assume it was. I was never told what would happen next, what the outcome was. The anxiety I lived through for my remaining two years in the Royal Navy was indescribable. I was offered no support, no counselling, and I'd just been emotionally pulped by those trained for wartime interrogation.

I was desperate to escape the knowing looks and buzz - and the increasingly nasty comments made to me by my warrant officer Bungy on watch. He continuously asked me if I had any ethics, read The Guardian, preferred 8's to a skirt, or had ever had a strapadicktomy (– naval imagery of lesbian activity using a strap-on dildo). So I applied for a swap-draft. This is a process whereby you can exchange your posting for someone of the same rank and branch, elsewhere. I applied to somewhere that nobody in their right minds would willingly go – BFFI – British Forces Falklands Islands.

The heat seemed to be turning up. There was an awful woman, Lieutenant Baker, Ma Baker to the rest of us, in line with the Boney M song, who was known for her strict discipline and general nastiness. She had called me in to an office one night shift, telling me she had heard rumours about me, and how I was brighter than most of the women on the watch, and not to be so stupid as to lie about who I was. I have no idea how she got this information – did she access my test records from my application to join the Navy? Clearly it was a shot across my bows. I had to keep my head down.

In the remaining stagnant months, I lived a double life, working hard, mixing with my team, gaining a promotion, and heading into London with Jane and Katy, to The Bell. But we were cautious. Katy would park her car about a mile from the base, I would jump on the tube for one stop and they would pick me up there. I swear that we had all experienced the rustling of leaves as we were out at times, even during the day getting some shopping. We firmly believed we were being followed.

I would occasionally go to the Drill Hall vegetarian café. According to 'The Pink Paper', which I'd managed to acquire on my cross-London travels and furtively smuggle into the base, it was a lesbian hangout.

I didn't even know what a vegetarian was. But the months I had exploring my new-found sexuality in the biggest playground the Royal Navy could've posted me to, London, were amazing. I snogged my first woman Donna, a posh arts student from Chiswick, after pretending to miss my tube home one night.

But most of all I loved The Bell. It was dark, it played great music, and I'd find myself standing at the bar with the likes of Jimmy Somerville of The

Communards. I knew nothing about gay culture then – bears, S&M, vanilla, all these terms sounded rough, scary, and dangerous. It was Emma who woke me up to these other worlds.

We had headed out one night in Katy's car, Jane had her leather jacket on. The only difference was that tonight, the audience were different. Desperate for a pee, I opened the door to the women's loo, only to be greeted by a leather clad woman on all fours, wearing a dog collar attached to a lead held by a woman wearing a WWII German Officer's cap. Whilst I was used to uniforms, this was a new one on me.

"She's my dog" the handler explained as they bimbled past me. Everyone in the loo, not that I looked around much as I was way too shy for that, was wearing something made of leather.

I darted back to Jane "everyone's wearing leather in ere..but you'll be alright, you've got yer jacket on" I said helpfully.

"Fuckin shite Maz" she exclaimed in her Auf Wiedersehn Pet North East accent, "it's fuckin S and M night."

"What the fuck was S&M?" I wondered

"Stay close guys" she told us. I did – I stayed close to Emma, a boyish Cockney I'd spied a few times in there. A few weeks, snogs, and fumbles later, I eventually stayed the night in her room in a woman's housing co-op, somewhere near the British Telecom tower. Nervous, excited, we got into bed, and she started to grind on top of me, and as I put my hand around her waist, my fingers went cold – handcuffs. What the fuck?

"What's these for?" I asked, even though it's fucking obvious.

"Oh, come on, you Forces people like a bit of rough and a bit of role play don't yer?" she answered. Panicking, I then noticed black and white fetish photos on every wall.

"No, No, I don't want this" I said politely

"Tough shit" she answered, locking the door, trying to pin me down and reaching her hand into a tub of KY jelly underneath the bed.

Luckily, I was fit. I pushed her off with all my strength, and climbed out of her window, and dropped down, luckily she was on the lower floors, and I ran and ran until I hit a main road somewhere near Euston station, and as I did, my knight in shining armour appeared – the Vietnamese cash-in-hand taxi driver we'd used to take us back to base from The Bell on many occasions.

I arrived at the main gate.

"You dirty slapper, Maz!! Grinned one of the approving Royal Marines. I couldn't smile back.

"What's up Maz, had a good sesh did we? You look like you've seen a ghost love" noted another over his brew.

I never saw Emma again, but years later, her photo was on the cover of an S&M magazine in a gay bookshop. I had naively thought that only men raped women.

In December 1990, I was walking through the base when a voice shouted from the window of an office block.

"Oi Maz, you're draft's in" shouted Helen, a fellow radio operator.

"What?"

"Yep, they'll tell yer later, yer goin JCUFI."

"What's that?"

"Joint Communications Unit Falklands Islands."

By Christmas, my Mum and Dad had moved again. My Brother had had a child out of wedlock after buying himself out of the Royal Navy. And the reality of my situation was hitting me hard. I had to talk to my family.

Standing at a cash machine with my Dad, as my Mum eyed the decorated shop windows further down, he asked

"Got yerself a husky sailor yet?"

I froze, keeping my back to him, my heart pounding. I was used to my late Great-Gran asking the old fashioned "Are you courting?" question, but what do I do here?

"No Dad, I'm not interested, I want my career."

I could feel his eyes boring into the back of me. And then the floodgates opened. I told him how I was gay, that I'd been investigated and how I was going to The Falklands for four months.

"That's bloody brilliant love"

"What?" I asked.

"Well, I knew there was something wrong like. But there's no pregnancy and no wedding to pay for. That's bloody brilliant news!" He exclaimed.

In a daze, we caught up with my Mum, who was having a ciggy on a steel bench. Seeing my red eyes, she asked what was wrong.

"Have you two had a bloody row again? It's bloody Christmas you know" she nagged.

"No, no we haven't.... Mum, I..." I started, until my Dad told me I didn't have to tell her anything. "No. If you know, then Mum deserves to know too." From there it tumbled out.

My Mum, despite what she felt, never rejected me, or told me I was a disappointment. She was always brilliant with my future partners. Bizarrely, I had never been a heavy drinker, we couldn't afford it at home and certainly not spirits. But I mumbled my story whilst drinking the entire top row at the bar of whatever pub we had ended up in. Suffice to say, I was assured I was loved, no matter who I was.

At the same time, although I didn't know it, Jane and Katy were dismissed from the RAF and Royal Navy respectively. As part of that investigation, all eyes had again turned to me. Someone had seen me getting into Katy's car.

Luckily, I got drafted. I had a night at RAF Brize-Norton, but the plane that was due to take us to the Falklands had caught fire, and so we had to head back to base. This happened another time, so we were accommodated overnight, much to the joy of a drunken RAF sergeant who repeatedly harassed me outside my door all night, and on most of the flight there. Luckily, I was so knackered I conked out, and avoided sitting next to him as I found a seat next to a cargo load.

RAF Mount Pleasant was the base I arrived at. As far as my experience went, the Royal Navy may as well have drafted me to Soho, the UK's main sex locale. Whilst many of the heterosexual men based there, were sexually frustrated, away from wives and girlfriends, I was having the time of my life. Royal Navy friends on the base were considered gold dust, largely because we knew when the ships would come in, and that meant beers and parties. So I got courted in more ways than one; helicopter rides up mountains, ships parties, miner-themed dos in rooms decked out with bin bags. as men doubled up to share bunks between shifts, freeing up a room to make way for a hidden bar. Raves were held in aircraft hangars decked with netting and lights. After my 21st birthday party, I ended up with a female Army corporal in bed above a pub in Port Stanley.

Nobody gave a shit. Rules were more relaxed there. Everything underhand was done by word of mouth. Some guys had found magic mushrooms and were partying at weekends on the paradise of unspoiled beaches lining the island - I got a wildlife holiday - in all respects, that I'd never have had back home.

The double standards prevailed. Men would sexually harass women at all times of day and night. It was something integrated and unchallenged in the culture. It was a fierce place too - fights would break out between regiments seeking to settle old scores, and you'd have to skip over the dried blood on the concrete floors when heading to breakfast. Lesbian sex was hidden and covert, in broom cupboards, snatched moments on hidden mattresses in untouched corners. I had the most sexual time of my life. I dated Teri, a cute Army postwoman, who, when asked by one of my oppos why she liked me and not a bloke, told them it's because I had a cute little boy face. And I did, at the time.

My attempts to rise above the harassment weren't always met with success.

"Like a bit of black, do you?" demanded three Royal Navy sailors from HMS Active one night when I danced with a lovely black guy from my watch.

"Hey Maz, we've heard you swing both ways, is that right, cos we just wanna know like? We won't think bad of you" three other radio operators asked me.

One night following a quiet shift and after that, a quick fuck in the toilets, our Army corporal Anita, pointed her finger at me and my latest conquest, and beckoned us to come over. Red faced and sure that she had realised the reason for our climaxed expressions, we were taken into a stairwell as we were walking back to our quarters.

"Fucking watch yourselves. The SIB landed in a helicopter today. They're here on the Islands."

It always amazed me how the straight men and women whom others assumed to be the biggest slappers around, would always be the most at ease with their gay colleagues.

"I don't give a fuck" she continued. "But don't lose your fucking careers girls."

So, we watched out for ourselves. This time, the SIB weren't visiting me. During my time there, I witnessed a straight couple having oral sex on duty, as did my entire watch, yet of course, nobody acted on it. Double standards yet again.

On the last morning of my tour, I awoke to a plethora of small gifts left for me during my sleep, by my various encounters, whom I'd never see again. There I was, a serious military person in uniform, carrying my kit bag and rucksack towards the humming Hercules transporter plane, with an armful of girly cuddly toys.

I still have mementoes of my time there, a 21st plaque dotted with cap badges and Falklands coins, made for me by the Royal Engineers from bits of scrap brass and metal they'd found, and tea towel signed by fellow party goers and signed by many who were dykes in disguise.

I'd certainly done my bit for inter-service relations, and enough to be recommended for advancement.

I'd done so well, in fact, that I had applied and been accepted for, officer training. I just had to wait my turn to be called to attend Britannia Royal Naval College.

Scuttled.

Scuttle – to sink a ship by opening her hull to the sea, letting water in, and scuttling her.

I had leave whilst awaiting my enhanced security clearance. I had to go through vetting procedures, ensuring I could handle highly classified and sensitive material. During my wait, an old schoolfriend phoned me unexpectedly one day. She'd found me because our mums had stayed in touch after we'd moved down to Oxfordshire. She told me she'd had a visit from a Mr Brown, who had proceeded to ask her questions about our school days together – was I political, did I drink heavily or do drugs, did I have debts, was I gay?

Luckily, I hadn't seen her for many years, so she wouldn't have known anything about my sexuality, but deep down, I was anxious and terrified. Presumably, this was the security services doing some digging. She described him as being Scottish and having a muzzy.

When I got back to HMS Warrior for a brief period, luckily any drama or enquires about me had died a death. No doubt they'd been replaced by goss about someone else. Most of those I knew had been posted elsewhere. One afternoon, I was asked to go over to one of the blocks and meet a Mr Johnson, as part of my vetting. Sat behind a table with an A4 leather folio, Mr Johnson proceeded to grill me about my enhanced security clearance, asking me precisely the same questions he'd asked my schoolfriend. He was also moustached and Scottish. Obviously this was the same bloke going by a different name.

At the end of this grilling, he closed his folio and rested his pen on top – then stared right into me. I felt clammy.

"If there's ever any element of doubt, we usually give the benefit of the doubt" he stated, his blue eyes holding fast and awaiting some reaction from me no doubt. He didn't get one. I wasn't socially aware enough, or as I discovered in my forties, I was too autistic to even pick up on any nuances he was hoping to get from me. But seemingly, he had decided I wasn't a dyke. Nevertheless, around this time, I started to hear clicks on my phone calls home too. Clearly, I was being observed.

A brief course at HMS Mercury with the United States Navy to learn sneaky-beaky stuff, I was finally despatched to RAF Edzell – an American spy base in Aberdeenshire, north Scotland. Its intention as I discovered years later, was to spy on the Chinese. I was never told that.

In the Commcen were posters outlining the values of the US military, which Royal Navy lads had addended with 'we also award copious medals for performing basic tasks'. Quite a laugh really. As one oppo said, the Americans did seem to get a medal for sending a signal or posting a letter.

Upon arrival, the luxury of the US lifestyle was apparent. My room had only one other bed in it apart from mine, a luxury. It was a large room, with fitted wardrobes and bathrooms, a mini bar and even a bottle opener. The base itself had a cinema and an incredible setup for scran; the galley had counters for bacon, pancakes, omelettes, croissants, and not a sniff of a cheesy-hammy-eggy anywhere.

Gaunt matelots arriving from tours with the Royal Navy would gain weight weeks after arriving. The more astute of them, realised that the Yanks loved anything UK related, so set about buying 35p gold badges from Royal Navy stores, creating designs on them with black marker pen, and trading them as exclusive or special forces badges, in return for vat coupons to buy goods from their NAAFI. Cue an array of gleaming British sailors heaving ghetto blasters and mountain bikes off shelves, at a fraction of the price.

Edzell was an odd place, a huge golf ball on a hill. The hills were six foot deep in snow, and my walks to work were via passing hares and hawks. It's the only time I got to wear my long, woollen Royal Navy winter coat. Sometimes I'd get a lift in a passing US Army jeep, but people were segregated. There were factions – as in the UK. US marines would have 'their' table for meals and black soldiers would sit together. I was told one night by the few Royal Navy guys serving there, told me that I was "one of their girls" i.e., that I should not make myself sexually available to any US sailor, marine or soldier.

No chance of that like. By this time, a pen pal back in Liverpool, had become my partner. There was a peace camp set up on the perimeter fence of the base, with a huge banner with "Top Secret Spy Base" painted onto it. The related women's peace camp Greenham Common was not known to me until many years later. The best entertainment was watching the women try and dig under the fence on one side, while American soldiers with spades filled the holes in from the other.

I'd also realised at this time, just how apart I was from attitudes in civvy street too. One day, at a small, local shop, in what was quite a Christian and conservative nearby village, I'd asked if they had a copy of Gay Times. The response was stammering, blushing and clearly embarrassed. I felt ashamed for asking.

As a result of the peace camp, which was occupied solely by women, and many lesbian women, the jokes about "the dykes" outside, were increasing on-watch. To pass the time on watch, male oppos would make jokes about wanting to go out and watch them have sex, or join in as a threesome, or show them what a proper dick looked like. Alternatively, they would ridicule them about their short hair and hippy clothes. My increasing discomfort at this, and not being able to speak out and defend them, was separating me from my uniform, my colleagues, and my identity.

I was getting dressed for night shift one night when I received a call in my room.

"Wren Maz?"

"Yes"

"Can you come to the main gate as soon as you can please?"

"But I'm due on night shift"

"No need, you're not going to work tonight, get changed and come over in your civvies."

I put the receiver down, I started to sweat under my woolly pully, shirt, and tie. Assuming I would be visited imminently by the SIB, I picked up all my partner's letters, ran into the shower and pulped them, pushing them down the shower's plughole in fear and desperation, tears melded with the hot spray.

I don't remember getting to the main gate, I guess fear and the human brain combine to shut down memory in some way. I was greeted by a Royal Navy SIB officer, a Scottish guy, and a civilian MOD police officer as a witness. Possibly a third person was there too. I was taken into a small room bedecked with US military paraphernalia, trophies, and a long, wooden table.

I couldn't take any more. The same questioning started, but far gentler this time. They'd intercepted my mail and there was a letter from my partner that I was forced to read aloud. Luckily, there wasn't anything sexual in it. Through snot and tears and the realisation that my life in the Navy was over, I told them everything they wanted to know – that I was in a stable relationship, how I went on weekend visits back to Liverpool. He told me to get my stuff and that he would drive me that same night, to HMS Cochrane – Rosyth Dockyard, in order to "keep me from the rumour mill."

What the fuck was he thinking? The Royal Navy had some of the fastest and most sophisticated telecoms equipment there was. How soon did he think my fellow signallers would let others know what had happened?

The journey down that dark night was cordial enough. The SIB officer told me that "he didn't want to do this, but it's my job." I have become aware that other SIB officers, forced to interrogate and dismiss us, have experienced mental health issues in later life. Maturity, life experience and reflection, mean they've realised their role in our human rights abuses.

He told me that it must be a relief for me, and in many ways, it probably was, but I wasn't feeling relieved. As we neared Rosyth and passed through Dunfermline, he took the liberty of showing me which pubs were the gay civilian ones, but told me to stick to my girlfriend back home.

Flotsam and Jetsam.

Flotsam and Jetsam – useless or discarded objects.

The squawking of shite hawks – Naval slang for seagulls, awoke me the next morning. I sat up. There were eight beds in the room, including mine, and all were empty. Clearly, I was in a room with those who work day shifts – writers, pen-pushers. I reported as required and was informed that I would basically be a skivvy, working in WRNS and Officers' quarters, a go-to person for accommodation issues and for collecting dirty laundry. This put me at odds with those with whom I shared a room, for if they were untidy or dirty, I'd be required to 'trash' their beds – a widespread practice of turning beds over and emptying bin contents onto them, to ensure they cleaned up their acts in future. I was bullied, confronted, and isolated, as a result.

I started to get asked why I was there – I seemed fit and healthy, why wasn't I in a Commcen? I felt increasingly concerned at night, fearful for my safety, fearful that they would turn on me and beat me up. I had no faith that should it happen, I'd be shown any support or sympathy - I'd had none so far. I made up a story that I stuck to – that my family were breaking up, and so I was being given a compassionate draft. But that fear of them finding out I was gay, and the prolonged wait of not knowing if and what would happen to me, and the ongoing bullying, broke me. I begged for my own room, which got granted after a few weeks. I spent many nights not knowing if the knock on the door was my final one or someone waiting outside to stove my head in. I wonder how many people who went through this, thought about suicide during that time? The forces didn't give a shit about you. It never entered my head, I was probably too introverted and unaware to even think of it, but I bet many did.

This isolation was intercepted by a grinning, lovely Brummie called Mike, who turned out to be an amazing oppo. He'd suffered a blow during karate onboard his ship, so was confined to desk duties until his balance and vision improved. He would be working with me. He kept schtum to me, despite later telling me he knew why I was there. Most of all, he accepted me and was kind. He got me out to the gym, and we rescued a kitten from a ship's cat together, fed it on a pipette he'd nicked from sick bay, and hid it in the quarters until it was strong enough for us to take to a rescue shelter. He also had a relative in Liverpool with whom he'd go to Everton games, so he would kindly give me lifts down and back at weekends to see my partner. I didn't have a car because I was still on a low wage.

As with all my other oppos, I never got to say goodbye to Mike. I was dismissed from the Royal Navy on 17th November 1992, after 2 years and 348 days service. The dismissal followed a routine medical where I was lined up outside sick bay amongst the homesick, the injured, the bed wetter's and anyone else the Navy didn't want. I was referred to as "a monster" by the dismissing medical officer. I was told I could take items of uniform with me, but all I could carry were a few things.

I returned home after a six-hour train journey, to Wrexham in North Wales. My Mum and Dad had moved into a one-bedroom council flat on a shit estate, so that my Mum could be nearer her Welsh family. I truly didn't understand the impact of what I had been put through. Nor did I know what was happening back home. I had often seen my Mum begging my Dad for cash for food when I was home on leave. She told me she had found a letter from another woman, thanking him for the gold chain he had bought her. Having me around would potentially risk exposing his dalliances. Who knows what strain my being there put him through?

He would kick off at me over something trivial, like changing tv channels, telling me he wished he'd had us aborted when he had the chance, that I would do as he says whilst I was under his roof and on one occasion after a row, telling me I should move to Liverpool with my gay mates with AIDS and die. My Brother had abandoned him after the birth of his own child, recounting tales of Dad protesting after he and his partner had asked him (Dad) not to attend the hospital, to give them time together. I'd also come home with Mike one weekend, to find my Mum trying to break up a fight between them. My Dad has not seen his son in all the 32 years since.

At no point did my parents encourage me to get myself on the housing register or seek counselling. We didn't come from a background that had that understanding. My Dad made some vague references to getting a solicitor, but there was no Equality Act then, nothing protecting gay people from discrimination. In any case, he'd only have the dosh for the bus, never mind a lawyer.

Salvage.

Salvage – to rescue a wrecked or disabled ship, or its cargo, from loss at sea.

Professionally, I have never recovered from what the Royal Navy did to me. Furthermore, it took me 30 years, and still some, to even begin to unpack and see, the devastation it rained on me. I took the first job I could, in a chippy at the end of the road, which was visited each night by gangs of armed lads with sinister expressions. And I did a government course where you could get your dole plus £10 a week.

Technological advances in the forces meant that at the time of my dismissal, software was replacing the hardware of teleprinters, flags, lights and morse code keyers. So it was a logical move to do a course in IT, as that seemed to be where things were going. Whilst some may think it was a wise move, the bottom line is, I had no choice.

I believe that at age 21, had I had some intervention around my career, I may have found a suitable alternative path. But I didn't. And 30 years later, I remain in unfulfilling work. After giving something your all, it is hard to find enthusiasm for second-best, although I have tried.

I would break down in tears in the jobcentre, when asked why I had left the Navy. I felt ashamed. They'd achieved what they set out to do - strip me of my self-respect, confidence, and human dignity. My nervous finger would point would-be employers at my discharge certificate – which merely read 'discharge shore' as my reason for leaving, which could be anything from alcoholism to home sickness.

When I *was* honest at interviews, employers would find reasons to reject me – I wasn't quite as strong enough as another candidate on a particular question, or I didn't show commitment. It was only 21 years after I was dismissed, that I discovered I had been medically discharged. Had I known, I could have deflected the outward, but not the inward, shame I experienced, by just telling them I was medically discharged, but no doubt that would lead to further questioning as to what for?

I returned to Liverpool in 1993 to live with my partner in a slug-filled, damp student house. I'd acquired a place on an HND course at Liverpool John Moores University by doing what veterans do – turning up smartly dressed and doing their homework. I was elated to be offered a place. LJMU was a poor man's Uni, a former polytechnic, but it felt as good as if I'd gotten into a red brick – not that I knew what one was until years later.

As I walked down the steps of the sweeping, neoclassical Mountford Building, facing the Mersey Tunnel, I raised my hands towards the Liver Birds in elation! It was the first time I felt I'd achieved anything since dismissal.

I worked hard and, in all honesty, I could've been on any course at any Uni, I was just happy to be there. At the end of my second year, I was offered a transfer over to the degree course, which I accepted without fully appreciating the financial burden it would leave me with. The poverty differences were stark again; I was the only one on my course without a laptop, so weekends were spent hiking across the various University buildings in the city to try and locate a library space with a free computer. I had to work, unlike others on my course, and did so at a local fried chicken outlet. My 'I'm a hickory chick' t-shirt would be the source of amusement for bevvied, post-match football fans. On top of this, my partner decided she was straight. She turned, overnight almost, into a heterosexual stereotype; wearing heels and make-up, and shagging a married bloke who had a baby on the way – in our bed.

I moved into the single spare room as I couldn't afford to move out and spent a lonely summer there with chickenpox. I eventually met another woman, from my course, who I loved very much but for whom I was just a fling. Sadly, her background reflected the poverty of my own, having a comfortable home and a car to sit in before exams. By contrast, I would sit gratefully out of the rain in the Irish Centre with a wet. She also wouldn't come out of the closet.

I also began to realise just how unaware I was, of civvy gay culture. The Liverpool Echo is a daily, local newspaper, and on a Saturday, there would be a football edition – called the Pink. One of my Uni mates had mentioned that you could buy the pink paper at the newsstands in the city centre, and I had naively gone there seeking what I thought was the gay weekly.

During this time, my Dad had announced my parents' divorce. Brilliant fucking timing as usual, just six months before my finals. He sat me down and coldly presented the facts as a mutual decision. Mum sat stony faced and numb. She'd lost her Mum, Brother, Dog, and pet cockatiel all within six months, and now she was losing her husband.

Graduation day was fantastic. My Mum, my flatmate Dave, and my then-girlfriend Lynn were there. My Mum couldn't afford the train fare from Wrexham, I'd posted it to her, and I had to pay for the rental of my mortar board and gown, and for the photos afterwards. But it was a special event and held in the grand Anglican cathedral in Liverpool

After graduating, I had an assortment of house shares and moves. Whereas my university friends were taken on holiday by family, I signed on the dole. I didn't have the connections others had to get a job. I rented a flat away from the city and lived with another woman for a few years. She proposed to me, but then conveniently forgot once her employer, aware that she'd been to Oxford University, sponsored her to do a Masters in Business Administration.

I on the other hand, was going nowhere.

Christmas 1999 was lonely, I went out into Liverpool on the New Year's Eve, alone, bumping into people who knew me but who failed to extend any warmth. I spent the night watching the millennium gig up at St George's Hall and resigned myself to leaving my home city. It's a fact that veterans often find it hard to settle, after a life on the move.

I lived with my Mum briefly. She had decided to leave Wrexham, realising the family she thought would be there for her weren't. She'd taken a flat on a crap estate in Stockport, to be near my Brother, who promptly then moved to Scotland. That time gave me a renewed connection with her, and a better understanding of what she had been through. She told me that the person I was after leaving the Royal Navy, was not the same person who had joined up. Clearly, she had seen a huge change in who I was. She also described how the photo on her sideboard of me in my uniform, would topple over repeatedly during the time I was being investigated. She'd instinctively felt that something was up. The supernatural was and always will be, part of our family lives. I just hope that if and when we get justice, she will see it from beyond the grave.

Like so many who serve, you push your feelings away. You focus forwards on the task. It's only in quiet or alcohol-fuelled moments, that you get to make sense of what happened to you. I was no different in that way.

After starting a job in IT in Manchester, which I hated, and after being bullied at work by a Jehovah's Witness, I escaped it to do trade union work, eventually becoming a branch officer. From there I worked as a diversity manager for a police force. Whilst I enjoyed it, it exposed me to some uncomfortable truths about my life – how free school meals had been an indicator of poverty, my own discrimination and lack of early life chances generally. I moved into the same role performance managing 33 NHS Trusts for a Strategic Health Authority. But then austerity kicked in, and so organisations cut down on nice-to-do activities. That happened alongside major NHS restructuring, I was unemployed. I did some short-term training and contract work, including work at a national level on diversity. However it appeared that the higher up I got, the more privileged and out of touch, my colleagues seemed to be.

It has been an ongoing source of amazement ever since, how employers would tell me that I didn't have enough experience to be a diversity manager, when actually I had first-hand, lived experience of discrimination, disadvantage and exclusion.

I went on to do a conversion course in Law and was offered a place at Chester College of Law. Despite having achieved the academic qualification even though working full-time, I couldn't afford to go. I would have loved to have studied human rights law academically. I wonder if it would have been helpful to me, psychologically, at the time. I had started to notice triggers, flashbacks, and reminders of my interrogations, and these continue until today. For example, when a colleague approached me in the office from behind, the panic and anxiety would start. I flashed back to the shouting and pacing and abuse from behind me during interrogation. Remembrance Day events with people in uniforms would find me uncontrollably breaking down in tears without warning. Meetings with a manager or anyone in power, in a shut room, would result in me sweating and feeling panicky. Worst of all, is seeing the Armed Forces march at Pride events, it is hurtful, opens up the old wounds and causes psychological distress, as you feel you are just someone on the outside watching everybody else sit at the table, knowing it could have been you.

At work, I have been unable to socialise, keeping myself to myself, learned behaviours from my early career. As I don't come from a background that knows how the world works, I was happy to challenge everything. When you've spent your life fighting, you're unlikely to just go with the flow anymore.

I attempted to find a suitable alternative career by visiting the adult careers service for software profiling of my skills, interests, motivations, and personality. Tests found that my most suitable career was an armed forces officer! I left after the session and sobbed and sobbed, uncontrollably.

The continuous ping-ponging of starting a job, not being able to hold it down due to mental health, grief at the fact I should not have ever been doing those roles, has continued into my fifties. It's resulted in constant house and city moves, and feeling constantly unsettled.

My diagnosis with autism in 2012 was as enlightening as it was disturbing. The diagnosis made me realise just how the well-structured environment of HM Forces, was highly suitable for an autistic person such as me. I have never found such a suitable environment since.

I achieved a war pension in 2012 for depression, and later received a diagnosis of PTSD, but have had no real support and no benefits awarded for this.

The discrimination I have faced, by public and private sector employers because of my disability, and my accent, particularly in the digital sphere, has been incredibly hurtful, triggering those experiences of my earlier discrimination and bringing it all to the surface again. Their attitudes have highlighted how the 'disability confident' scheme and public sector equality duty, are nothing short of farcical. There are workplace situations where you can be deployed to different projects with different managing organisations that lack central oversight of the implementation of adjustments. There are other situations when you're recruited by private sector organisations to work on public sector projects, with no mention of adjustments through the entire contractual process. I have taken cases to thirteen employment tribunals in 20 years. No doubt it's some way of hitting back at that earlier discrimination in my life, during which we had no laws to protect us. These repeated difficulties have left gaps on my CV, because I've been devoid of any firm career path or period of settledness after the Royal Navy trauma.

Another period of homelessness following a breakup of a relationship in 2010, saw my Mum sleeping on the couch of her one-bedroom flat, sacrificing her bed for me. After a few more moves, including renting a social housing flat in which I had no carpet, no furniture and plastic crates for table and chairs, and a Winter going to a food bank and spending days and nights sitting and sleeping on my kitchen floor, with just one radiator on, wearing a woollen hat and puffa jacket, in desperation, I turned to a women's housing co-op in another city. With just a week's money left before more homelessness, I moved to Edinburgh in 2016. One week later, my Mum died of a brain haemorrhage, completely unexpectedly. I had spoken to her just hours earlier. So, there I was, near to my last great loss at Rosyth - my Naval career, living just a few miles down the road in Fife, experiencing another great loss and more isolation.

Suffice to say, the housing setup was anything but co-operative. I had no time to grieve, I was alone, with no support and unemployed. I ran up debts in the course of getting down to my Mum's flat in Stockport, which I had to clear out single handed, and to get to her funeral in Wrexham. I was also bullied where I was living.

I moved into several house shares – one with a schizophrenic drunken Australian, another with a woman who didn't show up and left me sitting outside with all my belongings and I was eventually offered a social housing flat but endured endless sleep disturbance there from electric guitars and drunken neighbours in the block.

I must have sat in that flat for months, drinking, numb, grieving and alone, I had been performance managed out of another job, despite my work getting good feedback, and I don't believe I have ever recovered from this time. The worst thing is, my Mum never got to see me achieve justice.

A friend offered me a room in her house, so I stuck my stuff into storage and regained some sleep, fresh air, and balance back into my life, but despite us getting along well, this didn't last long. In 2018, aged 47 and still house-sharing, I was homeless again. Her wealthy lesbian friends had awoken her to how desirable Edinburgh was as a tourist destination, for the Fringe festival, tattoo, and castle; they'd encouraged her to make more money via renting my room out on Airbnb.

I was alone the first Christmas in 2016 after my Mum's death. Nobody in my family wanted to know, not my Dad who was alive, nor my Brother. Thankfully, I'd made friends with a Glaswegian guy called Jim, who had also lost his Mum. I had him for company during the Christmas day at least. The following year, just after I was given notice to leave the house share, I was invited to my Brother's house 300 miles away, for Christmas lunch.

"Just fuckin' chill out, it's xmas" he said to me in the pub on Christmas eve. He didn't understand, or want to understand, the terror and fear of homeless that I was feeling. I truly had nowhere to go. I did my best to put a smile on for him and his wife. After a merry Christmas eve of drinking and singing, the atmosphere soured as he threatened to put the Christmas dinner over my head the next day, just for offering to let his dog out for a pee. After confronting him on boxing day, I never saw him again. He dropped me a few months later, clearly viewing me as a burden. I can only assume he had reached the end of his capacity to cope with my ongoing distress over the years, following my life being smashed apart.

I had mentioned to my Mum over the last few months that I found his comments increasingly hurtful. He'd told me how I "needed to get my shit together", "stop being a rolling stone". Clearly he was oblivious to my attempts to pick myself up from what had happened to me, and start life again.

So, it was January 2018, I was homeless at 47 years of age, and an orphan in just about all respects – no close friends, no family contact, no job, and no home. Not the life I would have had had I been in the Navy.

Bizarrely, it was the Royal Navy connection that came to my aid. As a veteran, there was a hostel I could go into in central Edinburgh, so I narrowly avoided being on the streets by weeks. Unwittingly, I thought that this could be happening for a reason. Perhaps it was a homecoming, I would connect and make some veteran friends again, have a community and gain some support, but I was way off the mark. The hostel was an unsafe place, no CCTV and a rabbit warren of corridors which became playgrounds for the nightly fights, parties, drug dealing and visiting prostitutes. Sleep was impossible, and I would often pass someone's room only to see them sat in a chair with a needle stuck out of their arm. Some had their faith, or family, to see them through. Many of the Scottish veterans resented English veterans being there. During the regulated mealtimes there were daily fights. I also experienced harassment and hate crime – a dog woof shouted from an anonymous window as I crunched across the car park, post-it notes stuck on my door. They told me to fuck off, that I was a queer and that I looked like a man.

The police didn't want to know, They'd clearly marked the hostel as a no-go zone. The situation was desperate. I was a gay woman amongst men that the armed forces didn't want, I had no money and was in danger of losing the job I'd got with a large IT consultancy, through lack of sleep. I was offered a move to Dundee, but I'd still be amongst veterans, and believed I would get the same treatment. I did get to make a few friends, but we lost touch after I made a fresh start in July 2018 with the patient and understanding woman, who is now my wife.

During my time there in the hostel, I again saw the double standards applied to heterosexual veterans as opposed to homosexual ones, this time in terms of benefits. I heard how one married veteran had got a cheap married quarters with his wife, even when he had his own property, and he'd rented that out to get his mortgage paid, without telling his superiors. Gay married veterans would not have been offered this. I saw veterans who were drugged and boozed to their eyeballs, get Personal Independence Payments for their mental health. Yet there was me, denied this money despite my lack of addiction, even though I too had been diagnosed as having mental health problems, like these veterans.

So, one sunny Saturday that year, I made a fresh start in a small van paid for by the charity, guarded by its support workers, as my few bin bags were loaded up.

My workplace experiences have not changed. At the time of writing, in 2022, yet another employer has failed to make adjustments, and I am unemployed.

When I have applied for roles, say, in the civil service, I am asked on their application form if I have ever been dismissed from employment. Subsequently, 30 years later, I still am forced to carry that stigma, and disclose it, as if it is something I should be ashamed of.

The purpose of revealing my story is to intentionally tell it like it was, and is, for me, and thousands of others, who were treated so appallingly by their country.

I want to go beyond the ban and illustrate the ongoing effects of it and to put a stop to the bullshit I hear or read that everything is alright now that laws have changed, and you can be who you want to be. It isn't.

SITREP.

It's 30 years since my dismissal. At the time of writing, 2022, there is an independent government review into the experiences of LGBT+ veterans, which concludes in 2023. However, it contains no provisions for either compensation, or prosecutions for the human rights abuses we were subjected to. In other words, all the government are committed to doing is reading a report.

Apparently, the ban had stemmed from a group of Cambridge University students who had spied for the Russians during the cold war. But in applying such a ridiculous ban, the government risked creating the very animosity towards the United Kingdom that it had tried to nail.

Whilst the rest of the community were dancing to the Pet Shop Boys and Erasure, thousands of good people who had stepped up to serve their country, were stripped of everything they had. The zealousness with which the policy was implemented, is a shocking and degrading period of British military history.

I have since learned of people who were electrocuted, raped repeatedly via intrusive medical examinations, who have never worked again, who continue to self-harm, who were imprisoned, and forced to walk in straight lines around parade grounds, beaten up, and had medals ripped from their uniforms in front of their ship's companies or regiments. In some ways, I got off lightly.

There are other LGBT+ veterans who went through the same interrogations of course. Not all of us had the same experiences post-dismissal; many went back to homes that could afford to house, feed, or emotionally support them. Some people were in London and could group together to support and campaign on the issue, such as those who formed 'Rank Outsiders', the forces support organisation. I had no such support, and campaigned alone.

I organised a petition to Parliament, using Facebook to contact everyone from gay men's choirs to veterans, I wrote a letter to the Guardian in 2008. In 2022, my home city recognised me, as I was awarded one of the first Liverpool Echo's Rainbow List awards. This meant more to me than any medal I could have achieved. I broke down and cried when I got this.

I wrote to the Queen before she passed away, asking if I could wear the cap badge of the rank I would have achieved, had I not been discriminated against. She passed it to the Secretary of State for Defence, who in turn passed it to Navy Command. They told me no, I can't.

In 2000, the Ministry of Defence lifted the ban. To much pomp and circumstance down in London they apologised for our treatment. I certainly didn't get invited, nor know anything about it at the time. Me and probably loads of others.

In 2007, the MOD apologised again, and again, I didn't know anything about it. In 2020, the MP and Secretary of State for Defence, Johnny Mercer, also apologised. Not one person I know of, knew of this watery pile of shite. If they really wanted to, the government could find us, at least some of us, for example the campaigners and those, including myself, that took the UK government to the European Court of Human Rights. However, I think leaders would rather have a safe pair of hands who won't rock the establishment, which I discuss in a bit.

22 years have now passed since the ban was lifted. Yet still successive governments have done fuck all to repair these historical injustices. This 2022-23 review does not commit them to do anything rather than read a report, and the bottom line is, it is too little, far too fucking late.

THE MOB.

'MOB – slang for The Armed Forces'

So, what of our relationship with the military?

Bottom line is that the military have been happy to turn up at Pride events and marches, and to do all this apologising. But none of it has reached our ears. We haven't been invited to take part with them. In the past couple of years the Royal British Legion and Fighting with Pride i.e. charities, have invited us to take part, but not the services directly. In other words, nicely deflected and fuck all effort from them.

None of this bollocks has restored the shattered lives we still live. I believe the military should be banned from attending all Pride events until they get off their arses and restore as much of what we lost as they can. This is doable.

So what did we lose? Our human dignity, our self-esteem, our careers, homes, friends, pensions, medals or badges, like good conduct and long-service awards, resettlement grants and support. In other words, everything. I know one guy who served in the RAF, did his entire time and just around 6 weeks before, he was dismissed, he lost everything. Another guy had to give up his dog because he too, lost everything.

In all honesty, initiatives like the Armed Forces Covenant, signed up to by prospective employers of veteran's talent, have meant little in practice to us gay veterans. Employers have no real understanding of the internal and external, effects of the ban that multiply post-dismissal, nor do they give a shit. Even other veterans have not wanted to acknowledge that a poof could be as able, qualified, and integrated as other sailors, soldiers, airmen or women.

Some of my original oppos from HMS Raleigh did get in touch. It was clear I'd missed a reunion a few years earlier, which saddened me, and reignited the hurt again. But my experiences of service life were at odds with theirs. So there is little common ground, other than some funny memories, on which to connect. I am not sure how I would feel about seeing them now.

Since leaving the Navy, or rather, it leaving me, I hadn't considered myself a veteran. For me, the term meant someone injured in battle. But as I explored more, I finally started to embrace myself after all the rejection. In recent years I've applied for a veteran's badge, discount card and railcard; these are small acts of reclaiming some identity. I also bought a cap badge and beret, which I wore at my stepdad's funeral. And I started banking with a military bank. These are simple things that the government could have reached out to us about, to start the healing. Of course, they didn't.

Anyway, even if I wear a beret, it doesn't take away the anger I feel at not being able to wear the rank I should have achieved.

Most sickeningly, I have seen other LGBT+ veterans trotted out as poster boys or girls, for Veterans Gateway, the UK first point of call for veterans and their loved ones, as part of their Pride celebrations, only to discover that some of these veterans actually had a role to play in our interrogations, as ex-Military Police. It is no secret that many LGBT+ people in the service police, interrogated their own. Quite why the prime point of contact for UK veterans' welfare and advice, decided to use a former interrogator to celebrate pride, rather than tell an inspiring story of dismissed veterans and how we have attempted to rebuild our lives, is something only the government can answer.

Successive governments have left it way too long to do anything. As a result, stances have hardened. Any attempts now to pretend everything is ok and we are welcome back, is nothing other than a whitewash.

The Ministry of Defence has made it clear that veterans who had medals taken from them, can now have them returned. This was not from any act of goodwill – it stemmed from yet another, legal challenge by yet another veteran, to get his medals back. The claim was conveniently covered up in subsequent publicity.

We must ask ourselves why, despite the independent review that is taking place between 2022 and 2023 into our experiences, this has taken 22 years to initiate, since the ban got lifted?

Basically, they've not given a shit, and my view is that they want to do to us, what they did to the miners, the Hillsborough families or anyone else who is brave enough to question – hope that we will die off and go away.

Then came the fun and games of my reaching out to veterans' charities. This reaching was not the other way round, I have to add, because many of these charities didn't give a shit about us either or were staffed by ex-forces homophobes who could easily deflect any attempt by us to get support.

Existing and well-established charities now have policies which are allegedly non-discriminatory. But basically, it's a pile of shite when it comes to implementation on the ground.

My first baby steps of trying to re-join the military family, as a veteran, did not go well. I was full of hope of restoring something of the lost camaraderie, when I attended a course in 2018 for service leavers and veterans, run residentially by a well-known and established charity, to help find some career direction.

I was delighted to be on this course. Sadly, on day one I witnessed schoolboy homophobic "banter". This was devastating, because it was such a huge step for me to take. I'd thought times had changed. I raised this with the trainers, even though the banter wasn't directed at me. They told me that I was "in a military environment". I pointed out that not a single person on the course was in the military. And I left. The sense of pain and rejection again, by the military family, was stark and upsetting. It crushed me. This was such a huge step for me to have taken, only to get more of the same.

I then decided to join my local Royal British Legion and Royal Naval Association branches. Whilst I acknowledge there are some good people in these. But by and large, they seem to be an excuse by many veterans, usually white men, to resort to inappropriate behaviour at meetings, keep it as a clique or old boys club. Some expect that you are still the person you were when you joined up, or want to wear 'rig of the day', or stand up for the national anthem, other individuals think that sexist jokes and homophobic 'banter', is still alright, because they come from a culture when that was ok during service. Not exactly welcoming for me and my wife.

At veteran's socials or events, I found myself often asked how long I had served for. Upon providing an honest answer, I was told I am a lightweight for leaving the services early. Again, this is cutting and extremely damaging, as I didn't choose to leave early. And I am then put in situation of coming out and experiencing rejection, or ridicule, whichever way it goes.

I know of another veteran who was dismissed, She went to her local Armed Forces Day event, only to be told by a former Military Police Officer that he used to enjoy kicking queers out. Fuck all has changed, basically.

When I have engaged in programs, they're attended or facilitated by, people who lack the skills to challenge the sexist chats, homophobia or other small-minded tribal mindsets, that military culture encourages. The development of the tribal mindset is key to a well-functioning regiment, ship or squadron, and Veterans' events are just an excuse to return to exactly that.

The most damaging experience I have had though, is with a charity set up to allegedly, to support LGBT+ veterans such as I – Fighting with Pride.

This is a charity run by two-former officers; one ex-Royal Navy, who came out on the day the ban got lifted, and the first transgender oficer to openly serve in the RAF. Neither of them went through the interrogations we went through, neither of them lost their careers, and both of them worked on diversity initiatives, with much kudos and respect, in their respective service. One of them wrote a book about the ban.

I was shocked when I discovered that this charity had an interrogator, on their board – an ex Military Police Officer, as she said in her own account, had been part of investigations that resulted in dismissals of other gay personnel. It was well known in military circles that the SIB and Military Police, often contained gays that would kick out other gays. Quite why any dismissed veteran would feel comfortable going to a charity for support, when one of their potential interrogators was sitting on the board, is beyond me. They tried to justify this appointment when I pointed this out to them, rather than see the damage such an appointment could cause.

Whether it is this charity or another, the first mistake they make is to assume that dismissed veterans like me actually want to be part of the military family again. We do not want a gay version of Help for Heroes. Given the experiences we have already had with military charities, why would we bother?

The second mistake is to fail to ask us what it is we actually want. As a starting point we wanted a chance to talk to each other. For all those years, we haven't had the chance to talk to others like us, about what we went through, or to help make sense of our experience. And we are all in different places in terms of having had the time, or space, to process it, or not.

The third mistake is to assume that we all still respect the government or monarchy. These are institutions that, ultimately, sanctioned our dismissals. Whilst I took an oath some 30 years ago to serve the Queen, the bottom line is that I was never a Queen and country person, I joined up to get what I wouldn't have had at home, and I couldn't give a shit about them now – they sanctioned my dismissal.

When this charity was formed, I had hope – hope that we would be a campaigning group, direct and in your face. I believe that we should be out on the streets protesting. Look at what the Gurkhas did for their pensions. Look at the actions by the families of those who were experimented on at

Porton Down. However, it was soon clear that their aim was to support, not to get together the campaigners. It also became clear that via their networks, and their efforts, they had the ear of politicians, the military charities, and the press. Bloody interesting that not one of those entities came to speak to us directly. In my view, this is indicative of it being a bit of a closed shop in respect of those in power actually wanting to hear us out, much preferring a safe pair of hands that won't push too much.

Charities cannot seem to see that by suddenly doing an about-turn to welcome us back to the military family, they are also triggering our memories and experiences, and causing psychological distress and the re-living of our experiences. Whilst they mean well, they lack the psychological insight to assist. This in no way negates the positive impact they may have had for some individuals. But for some of us, we're only just starting to awaken to the reality of our situation. This has resulted in flashbacks and painful emotions.

The irony for me is that during the great wars, service men and women, and civilians and animals, fought for our democratic freedoms. That freedom includes the right to hold an opinion and express it. Yet it seems that military charities want us to pretend we are still loyal service men and women.

Well, we're not. We were betrayed by our country, not the other way round, yet I have repeatedly discovered that if you are a veteran who is not pro-monarchy or pro-government, you are ostracised and unwelcome, yet there is nothing in the charter or charitable purpose of these organisations that state you must hold a particular viewpoint, so in other words, they will indirectly, also breach your human rights to freedom of expression and freedom of though, conscience and religion, in excluding you, and I have had experience of that from more than one, military charity.

I initially supported Fighting with Pride; setting up a North East group for them, which they asked me to do. But I found I got no support in promoting it. I offered to help with their diversity and governance work, putting in a bid proposal for them, and doing TV interviews about my experiences. As time went on, I could see that the agenda was to not rock the boat, not to protest, and to forge links with the rest of the establishment. Incidentally that is not to say they are wrong, but the hope many of us would have had, would be to campaign on the streets. This has been eradicated.

They also appear, certainly to some LGBT+ dismissed veterans such as I, to be self-appointed representatives of our views, to government and military organisations.

Trips are often organised by charities, to enable veterans to visit the cenotaph, battlefields etc. Such events are undoubtedly well-meaning, but they have been organised without any thinking through of the emotional reactions that such events or even invitations, may trigger.

Despite being told that "It is all about you", in one engagement I had with this charity, there were no avenues for veterans to talk to each other, at first. Meetings consisted of monthly calls, controlled by the charity. This meant that instead groups of veterans started to set up their own WhatsApp and Facebook groups. The charity invited me personally to Downing Street. Apparently Boris Johnson wanted to hear about my story. The night before, I realised that it wasn't anything to do with this. was a Tory showpiece to illustrate how wonderful the UK was to be gay. I dropped out and returned the train fare the charity had given me, and in all honesty, I felt lied to. I also noticed a disproportionate number of politicians appear on the calls we veterans were pencilled in to attend.

When I announced, that I was going to try and obtain the records of my interrogations, the charity stepped ahead and told us that it was 'using its contacts' to find out what had happened to them. Cue a big TV campaign on BBC news to illustrate how the MOD had deleted them, and how they now wanted a meeting with the already-onside, Minister for Veterans, Johnny Mercer MP, to discuss this.

I cannot help feeling that the more critical of us, are being side-lined or controlled by military charities, and if we dare set up our own groups or expose what really went on, it gets crushed and brought back in – cordon, contain, control, is classic military thinking. In response to this particular aspect, I announced that our solicitors and the European Court of Human Rights, would still hold these documents that show what we were asked during interrogation. We could surely still get our paws on them – and publish them – so that the public knows exactly what their taxes were paying for those in uniform to do to us.

On another call I attended with other veterans, to which a guest speaker was invited, the guest was informed that we were all lamenting the death of the Queen. This wasn't true, I was certainly not lamenting the death of the person who ultimately, sanctioned my dismissal. Suffice to say, my punishment for this is that I am now blocked from viewing their Facebook page. I was ejected without reason, or explanation, from the calls with other veterans. When I complained, it took six weeks to get a reply. When I have asked for explanation, or examples, none were forthcoming. Why would I lament the death of someone who sanctioned the loss of everything I held dear in my life? Despite republicanism being a perfectly valid viewpoint, it has not stopped this charity from doing precisely what the Royal Navy did to me – breach my human rights. Such rights include freedom of expression and holding a viewpoint. The breach excludes me from the military community of similar veterans.

I expressed interest in marching at the cenotaph remembrance parade in November 2022. But I was informed, very late in the day and only upon asking, that I could not march as spaces were already taken. This rebuttal came despite the fact I had replied on the same day that spaces were first offered out. I was also not offered a ticket to the festival of remembrance or invited to the after-parade drinks reception. Yet I had stated I would like to attend, and none of them required attendance at the parade. After the parade, on TV coverage, I saw attendees who had already marched the previous year too, so there were spaces available after all.

Critical veterans are clearly not welcome and are excluded, by military charities, yet we have every reason to be critical and to feel betrayed.

Incidentally, I went to the festival of remembrance anyway, with my wife, in crackin' seats. We mixed with other veterans who were not gay, and who were absolutely wonderful people who listened to my experiences, without the usual dickhead banter or sweeping statements that all the Navy are gay.

Military charities, and the military, focus on the positive changes that have happened for serving gay men and women. But there's no attention paid to the hurt and anger that I and others, personally still feel. It also seems as though we are suddenly being courted, welcomed back to the military family, with the assumption that we were all psychologically, or politically, where we were 30 years ago. We aren't.

There is a boon generally, in those who have had service careers, seeking some cash once back in civvy street - a swathe of those who have written books, such as ex-special forces, or those who can't let go of the military and feel a need to work in, or establish, related charities. In all honesty, I believe some individuals have piggybacked on our experiences. They've written books and collected honorary degrees and OBEs as a result, but not gone through what we did. A number of us, myself included, can see right through this agenda.

Because of the passage of time, and my ongoing suffering, displacement, and lost life chances, I have pursued small acts of resistance against the establishment.

Like sections of my fellow Liverpool fans, I will not sing the national anthem or will boo it instead. It represents only the inequality, class differences and discrimination that my city, and I, have faced.

I will avoid buying British goods. If Britain doesn't want me, then it can kiss my arse in return. I got married in as far north of Scotland a location I could afford to get to, and certainly away from any military strongholds.

I can no longer engage with military associations or charities, no matter how many rainbow flags they put up or how many Prides they visit. I feel no pride whatsoever in the Union Flag. The monarch, as head of our Armed Forces, is the person who ultimately sanctioned our dismissals. This view, of course, will be unpalatable for some. For me, it's the only way I have a voice.

Do I speak for everyone who went through this? No of course not. And they won't all have the same slant on how they feel about the government, monarch or charities. But I bet I am not just the only one speaking from my heart with what I have said. There will be others who feel the same.

Do I live in hope for redress? Yes.

Am I living in la-la land? Probably. They've waited long enough to make it, and done fuck all. They know where we are and who we are, too.

Does it feel like it all happened yesterday? Definitely. We've been frozen in time.

I don't want or need, the fucking violins either.

Pipe Down!

Pipe Down – on sailing ships signals were given to the crew by sounding the boatswain's (bo'sun's) pipe. One such was 'piping down the hammocks' which was the signal to go below decks and retire for the night. Naval slang for 'Shut the Fuck Up.'

This is a good place to stop and highlight some of the awful comments, myths, and reactions that I've heard or seen over the years, usually from other veterans.

"You knew the rules when you joined up, so why did you join?"

In all honesty, I didn't know the rules. I had no idea what a homosexual was, I was an 18-year-old teenager. I certainly didn't know that I was one. At the end of the day, it was the rules, not us, that were at fault. Those rules were the equivalent of saying you can't serve in the forces if you ever get a grey hair, or you've got the wrong eye colour. The rules were deemed unlawful by a judgement in the European Court of Human Rights. That exposed the UK Government's behaviour towards us. It also wasn't just the existence of the rules, it as the disgusting way they were implemented. At the time I was dismissed, heterosexual service women who got pregnant also had rules applied to them – they were forced to leave, and that too, has been deemed illegal. But those women weren't' interrogated, imprisoned, humiliated. They didn't have their medals ripped from their uniforms.

"Why didn't you keep your gob shut and stay in the closet?"

The forces are unique in that being in them, is a way of life, not just a job. Your oppos are your family. Everything gets talked through and sorted between you. You go through a lot together. Coming out is a huge process for someone, no different than say a divorce. So why should some people be allowed to share their life shit if others can't?

"There was no torture, it was just an administrative discharge."

Bollocks. The Independent Review will capture the real experiences of what people endured. I know of people raped, beaten up, electrocuted and imprisoned. We will never know the extent of what went on, nor the true numbers affected, because people got kicked out differently. Some went to court martial and left 'services no longer required', some were discharged shore, or medically, and some left because they'd had enough. I am hopeful that the final government report, due in May 2023, shows the truth of what happened in the name of Queen and country.

"Why should you get compo, you chose to be gay?"

Being gay was never a choice. Being honest, if it were, it'd be far easier to be straight. There is no compo mentioned in the scope of the government review. We're still waiting for an apology, and we've lost everything – careers, pensions, homes, friends, our way of life, post-service reunions and ceremonies, careers and resettlement support, medals, good conduct and long-service badges, prospects, and human dignity. If that happened to you kid, friend, or family member, what would you want for them? Many of us suffer lifelong psychological harm from what happened. It took me about 20 years to look in a mirror again because of the shame the Navy made me feel about who I am.

Bibliography

LGBT veterans independent government review - About us - LGBT Veterans Independent Review - GOV.UK (www.gov.uk)

Records of Gay Military Sackings deleted by Ministry of Defence - Records of gay military sackings deleted by Ministry of Defence - BBC News

Royal Navy Careers 2022 - Royal Navy Jobs | Careers in the Navy & Royal Marines (mod.uk) P6

Glossary

Bevy – an alcoholic drink

Bezzy – best friend

Bimble – a leisurely walk

Brummie – a person from Birmingham

Buzz - gossip

Cheesy-Hammy-Eggy – a popular but simple, item on the menu in the Royal Navy, made from cheese, egg, ham, mustard, and bread

Civvy - civilian

Commcen – Communications Centre

Compo - Compensation

Dosh - Money

Goss - Gossip

Handkerchief code – the wearing of a particular colour, or placement, of a handkerchief, to non-verbally communicate a person's sexual preferences or fetishes

Lightweight – a person lacking depth, ability, or below average

LJMU – Liverpool John Moores University

Matelot – a sailor

Mob – slang term for the Armed Forces

MOD – Ministry of Defence

Muzzy – a moustache

NAAFI - Navy, Army, and Air Force Institutes, an organisation running canteens and shops for British service personnel

Oggy – hot dog

Oppo – a best friend in the Royal Navy

Pissheads – drunken people

Pit – a bed aboard ship

Polari – a secret language adopted by gay people

Provy – Provident; a credit union

Scran – food

Sesh - session

SIB – Special Investigations Branch; the name given to the detective branches of all three British military police arms: the Royal Navy Police, Royal Military Police and Royal Air Force Police

Slapper – a vulgar or course woman who has many sexual relationships

Sneaky-Beaky – a covert investigation

Spliff – a cannabis cigarette

Shipmate – a person aboard the same ship as you in the Royal Navy

Stand-off – the practice of allowing members of a shift to leave early

True dit – Naval slang for a qualification of a statement or story which sounds completely implausible. but which is true

Wet – a hot drink

Woolly Pully – standard issue navy blue, woollen Royal Naval jumper

WRAF – Women's Royal Air Force

WREN – popular and official term for a member of the WRNS

WRNS – Women's Royal Naval Service

8's – the working uniform of the Royal Navy, consisting of fireproof blue trousers, blue shirt, and a beret.

Printed in Poland
by Amazon Fulfillment
Poland Sp. z o.o., Wrocław
07 January 2023

813c860d-fe52-4810-94e8-1c375e8d8517R01